How I Taught My Kids to Read

S. V. Richard

How I Taught My Kids to Read

Part III
of IV

Four-Part Series
On Teaching Your Child to Read

By S. V. Richard

Copyright S.V. Richard 2022

*Published in 2022 by The Little
French eBooks*

INTRODUCTION

How I Taught My Kids to Read, Part III may be used to reinforce words learned through the second-grade. It is a step-by-step workbook that builds on the beginning literacy and first-grade words taught in *How I Taught My Kids to Read, Part I* and *How I Taught My Kids to Read, Part II*. A parent or teacher may use *How I Taught My Kids to Read, Part III* to refresh basic reading, writing, and computer skills with students. Ideas to individualize instruction or motivate students are also included with the activities.

The materials a parent or teacher will need to complete the activities are colorful poster boards, crayons/markers, index cards, tape, pencils, paper, a binder, and sentence strips. Optional materials include a three-hole puncher, glue, scissors, old newspapers, old magazines, craft jewels/gems, blank books, and a highlighter. In order to complete the optional technology piece, a computer and computer supplies will be needed.

Part One reviews primer and beginning literacy words. Part Two reviews words taught through the first-grade level. Part Three is geared toward second-grade level words; however, lower level words are also reviewed and a few higher level words are introduced. Part Four is geared toward a student reading on a third-grade level.

PRE-ASSESSMENT

Have the student _

1. Start a new board by choosing his or her favorite color poster board.
2. Write a title on the poster board, such as "My Second Grade Words".
3. Hang up the poster board.
4. Write his or her favorite hobby on an index card. For example, "fishing", "reading", "writing", "drawing", "dancing", "swimming", "baseball", "basketball", "collecting stamps", etc.
5. Tape the index card to the poster board.
6. Point to the index card and read his or her favorite hobby.
7. Complete the pre-assessment on the next page.

Tips to Integrate Technology

1. Type his or her favorite hobby on the computer.
2. Type the sentence: (Insert student's name) is (insert student's favorite hobby). *The sentence may need to be changed (from "is" to "will" or from "is" to "will play") to fit the chosen hobby. For example, "Richard is writing." "Richard will dance." "Richard will play basketball."
3. Print the document and place it in his or her binder.

Tips to Integrate Writing

1. Write his or her sentence on the sentence strip.
2. Hang up the sentence strip in a designated area.
3. Read the sentence off of the sentence strip.

Tips to Differentiate Instruction

1. Point to each word on a prewritten sentence as the parent or teacher reads it. The parent or teacher may choose this option if the student is unable or learning how to speak.

Tips to Motivate the Student

1. Insert graphics on his or her document that relate to his or her favorite hobby.
2. Make a collage of pictures from old newspapers or magazines showing his or her hobby.

PRE-ASSESSMENT

# of words identified correctly: +

Parent/Teacher Instructions: Write the student's favorite hobby by #1. Check off each word the student read correctly. Write the number of words the student read correctly in the box above. Refer back to this box at the end of Part Three. If the student read correctly more than 35 words, you may choose to work in Part Four for more challenging words.

Student Instructions: Read the words you recognize in each column.

1.
2. always
3. next
4. friend
5. people
6. family
7. turn
8. around
9. off
10. light
11. found
12. best
13. don't
14. wish
15. cold

16. small
17. because
18. made
19. about
20. another
21. looking
22. author
23. caught
24. taught
25. cook
26. cookie
27. cookbook
28. playing
29. riding
30. store

31. shopping
32. yard
33. crown
34. frown
35. town
36. brown
37. television
38. beach
39. sit
40. your
41. why
42. its
43. too
44. many
45. buy

ALWAYS

Have the student _

1. Write the word "always" on an index card.
2. Tape the index card to the poster board.
3. Point to the index cards and read "always" and his or her favorite hobby.

Tips to Integrate Technology

1. Type "always" on the computer.
2. Type the sentence: I always (insert student's favorite hobby). *The sentence may need to be changed (from "I always" to "I am always" or from "I always" to "I always play") to fit the chosen hobby. For example, "I always dance." "I am always writing." "I always play basketball."
3. Print the document and place it in his or her binder.

Tips to Integrate Writing

1. Write his or her sentence on the sentence strip.
2. Hang up the sentence strip.
3. Read the sentence off of the sentence strip.

Tips to Differentiate Instruction

1. Write "(Insert student's name) Sentences" on a piece of paper. For example, "Richard's Sentences". Punch 3 holes in the paper if needed. Place the piece of paper in the front section of his or her binder.
2. Write the date and the new sentence on a new piece of paper and place it in his or her binder every day.

NEXT

Have the student _

1. Write the word "next" on an index card.
2. Tape the index card to the poster board.
3. Point to the index cards and read "next", "always" and his or her favorite hobby.

Tips to Integrate Technology

1. Type "next" on the computer.
2. Type the sentence: The bike is next to the house.
3. Print the document and place it in his or her binder.

Tips to Integrate Writing

1. Write "The bike is next to the house" on the sentence strip.
2. Hang up the sentence strip.
3. Read the sentence strip.

Tips to Differentiate Instruction

1. Substitute different words for "bike", and write the new sentences on a piece of paper. Place the paper in his or her binder.
2. Cut out pictures of different objects that might be found around a house. Prewrite the sentence "The _____ is next to the house." Place the pictures of different objects in the blank and read the sentence. For example, "The (insert picture of) car is next to the house."

Tips to Motivate the Student

1. Draw a picture of a bike next to a house.

FRIEND

Have the student _

1. Write the word "friend" on an index card.
2. Tape the index card to the poster board.
3. Point to the index cards and read "friend", "next", "always" and his or her favorite hobby.

Tips to Integrate Technology

1. Type "friend" on the computer.
2. Type the sentence: My friend is tall.
3. Print the document and place it in his or her binder.

Tips to Integrate Writing

1. Write "My friend is tall." on the sentence strip.
2. Hang up the sentence strip.
3. Choose any sentence strip and read it.

Tips to Differentiate Instruction

1. Write a sentence about his or her friend on a piece of paper. Place the piece of paper in his or her binder.
2. Read, write, and type the sentence: Her friend is tall.
3. Read, write, and type the sentence: His friend is not tall. The parent or teacher may choose this option as an additional enrichment activity.

Tips to Motivate the Student

1. Draw a picture of his or her friend.

PEOPLE

Have the student _

1. Write the word "people" on an index card.
2. Tape the index card to the poster board.
3. Point to the index cards and read "people", "friend", "next", "always" and his or her favorite hobby.

Tips to Integrate Technology

1. Type "people" on the computer.
2. Type the sentence: The people are going to her house.
3. Print the document and place it in his or her binder.

Tips to Integrate Writing

1. Write "The people are going to her house." on the sentence strip.
2. Hang up the sentence strip.
3. Choose any two sentence strips and read both.

Tips to Differentiate Instruction

1. Write the words "The", "the", "people", "Are", "are", "going", "to", "his", "her", "my", "house", "school", a question mark "?", and a period "." on separate index cards. Arrange the cards to create different sentences.
2. Read, write, and type the sentence: The people are going to his house.
3. Read, write, and type the sentence: The people are going to my house.
4. Read, write, and type the sentence: The people are going to school.
5. Read, write, and type the sentence: Are the people going to her house?

FAMILY

Have the student –

1. Write the word "family" on an index card.
2. Tape the index card to the poster board.
3. Point to the index cards and read "family", "people", "friend", "next", "always" and his or her favorite hobby.

Tips to Integrate Technology

1. Type "family" on the computer.
2. Type the sentence: My family is here with me.
3. Print the document and place it in his or her binder.

Tips to Integrate Writing

1. Write "My family is here with me." on the sentence strip.
2. Hang up the sentence strip.
3. Choose any two sentence strips and read both.

Tips to Motivate the Student

1. Use a laser pointer with interchangeable heads to point to each word as it is read.
2. Collect a ticket when he or she successfully completes the assignments for the day. If his or her binder has a plastic pocket on the front, place the tickets in there for safe keeping. (Prizes may be redeemed for a specified amount of tickets.)

TURN

Have the student ‗

1. Write the word "turn" on an index card.
2. Tape the index card to the poster board.
3. Point to the index cards and read "turn", "family", "people", "friend", "next", "always" and his or her favorite hobby.

Tips to Integrate Technology

1. Type "turn" on the computer.
2. Type the sentence: It is my turn.
3. Print the document and place it in his or her binder.

Tips to Integrate Writing

1. Write "It is my turn." on the sentence strip.
2. Hang up the sentence strip.
3. Choose any two sentence strips and read both.

Tips to Differentiate Instruction

1. Read, write, and type the sentence: It is his turn.
2. Read, write, and type the sentence: It is her turn.
3. Read, write, and type the sentence: It is not his turn.
4. Read, write, and type the sentence: It is not her turn.
5. Read, write, and type the sentence: It is not my turn.
6. Read, write, and type the sentence: It is my turn next.

Tips to Differentiate Instruction

1. Say, "Words can have more than one meaning. In the sentence 'It is my turn.', the word 'turn' means people are rotating an order in which they go. The word 'turn' in the command 'Turn right.', on the other hand, means to partly move around in this case to the right."

Tips to Motivate the Student

1. Hide a prize. Write directions for someone to find it using the challenge words: "go forward", "go backward", "turn left", and "turn right".

AROUND

Have the student _

1. Write the word "around" on an index card.
2. Tape the index card to the poster board.
3. Point to the index cards and read "around", "turn", "family", "people", "friend", "next", "always" and his or her favorite hobby.

Tips to Integrate Technology

1. Type "around" on the computer.
2. Type the sentence: Please turn around.
3. Print the document and place it in his or her binder.

Tips to Integrate Writing

1. Write "Please turn around." on the sentence strip.
2. Hang up the sentence strip.
3. Read any three sentence strips.

OFF

Have the student _

1. Write the word "off" on an index card.
2. Tape the index card to the poster board.
3. Read the word "off".
4. Choose any three index cards and read the words.

Tips to Integrate Technology

1. Type "off" on the computer.
2. Type the sentence: Turn it off.
3. Print the document and place it in his or her binder.

Tips to Integrate Writing

1. Write "Turn it off." on the sentence strip.
2. Hang up the sentence strip.
3. Read any three sentence strips.

Tips to Differentiate Instruction

1. Draw a line across the middle section of a piece of paper. Label the top part "off" and label the bottom part "of". Write sentences in each part using the specified word. Place the paper in his or her binder.
2. Read, write, and type the sentence: Do not turn it off.

LIGHT

Have the student _

1. Write the word "light" on an index card.
2. Tape the index card to the poster board.
3. Read the word "light".
4. Choose three index cards and read the words.

Tips to Integrate Technology

1. Type "light" on the computer.
2. Type the sentence: Turn off the light.
3. Print the document and place it in his or her binder.

Tips to Integrate Writing

1. Write "Turn off the light." on the sentence strip.
2. Hang up the sentence strip.
3. Read three sentence strips.

Tips to Differentiate Instruction

1. Read, write, and type the sentence: Do not turn off the light.

FOUND

Have the student _

1. Write the word "found" on an index card.
2. Tape the index card to the poster board.
3. Read the word "found".
4. Choose three index cards and read the words.

Tips to Integrate Technology

1. Type "found" on the computer.
2. Type the sentence: I found the bike.
3. Print the document and place it in his or her binder.

Tips to Integrate Writing

1. Write "I found the bike." on the sentence strip.
2. Hang up the sentence strip.
3. Read three sentence strips.

BEST

Have the student _

1. Write the word "best" on an index card.
2. Tape the index card to the poster board.
3. Read the word "best".
4. Choose three index cards and read the words.

Tips to Integrate Technology

1. Type "best" on the computer.
2. Type the sentence: My best friend will call me.
3. Print the document and place it in his or her binder.

Tips to Integrate Writing

1. Write "My best friend will call me." on the sentence strip.
2. Hang up the sentence strip.
3. Read three sentence strips.

Tips to Differentiate Instruction

1. Read, write, and type the sentence: I will call my best friend.

Tips to Motivate the Student

1. Call his or her best friend.

DON'T

Have the student ‒

1. Write the word "don't" on an index card.
2. Tape the index card to the poster board.
3. Read the word "don't".
4. Choose three index cards and read the words.

Tips to Integrate Technology

1. Type "don't" on the computer.
2. Type the sentence: I don't know.
3. Print the document and place it in his or her binder.

Tips to Integrate Writing

1. Write "I don't know." on the sentence strip.
2. Hang up the sentence strip.
3. Read three sentence strips.

Tips to Differentiate Instruction

1. Say, "Don't means do not."
2. Say, "The mark between the 'n' and the 't' is called an apostrophe."
3. Write "I do not know." underneath "I don't know." Highlight "do not" and "don't".
4. Write "Do not turn off the light." underneath "Don't turn off the light." Highlight "do not" and "don't".

WISH

Have the student _

1. Write the word "wish" on an index card.
2. Tape the index card to the poster board.
3. Read the word "wish".
4. Choose three index cards and read the words.

Tips to Integrate Technology

1. Type "wish" on the computer.
2. Type the sentence: I wish you were here!
3. Print the document and place it in his or her binder.

Tips to Integrate Writing

1. Write "I wish you were here!" on the sentence strip.
2. Hang up the sentence strip.
3. Read three sentence strips.

Tips to Motivate the Student

1. Make a card to send to a grandparent or family member. Write "I wish you were here!" inside the card.

COLD

Have the student –

1. Write the word "cold" on an index card.
2. Tape the index card to the poster board.
3. Read the word "cold".
4. Choose three index cards and read the words.

Tips to Integrate Technology

1. Type "cold" on the computer.
2. Type the sentence: It is cold in here.
3. Print the document and place it in his or her binder.

Tips to Integrate Writing

1. Write "It is cold in here." on the sentence strip.
2. Hang up the sentence strip.
3. Read three sentence strips.

Tips to Motivate the Student

1. Cut out pictures of clothes he or she would wear in the cold, such as boots, jackets, etc. Glue the pictures to a piece of paper. Allow time for the glue to dry. Write a sentence or two about the pictures using the word "cold". Place the paper in his or her binder.

SMALL

Have the student _

1. Write the word "small" on an index card.
2. Tape the index card to the poster board.
3. Read the word "small".
4. Choose five index cards and read the words.

Tips to Integrate Technology

1. Type "small" on the computer.
2. Type the sentence: I found the small box next to the book.
3. Print the document and place it in his or her binder.

Tips to Integrate Writing

1. Write "I found the small box next to the book." on the sentence strip.
2. Hang up the sentence strip.
3. Read three sentence strips.

Tips to Differentiate Instruction

1. Choose the small objects from precut pictures of small and large objects. Place the pictures of the small objects under the heading "small". The parent or teacher may choose this option if the student is unable or learning how write or use scissors.

Tips to Motivate the Student

1. Cut out pictures of small things. Glue the pictures to a piece of paper. Allow time for the glue to dry. Write a sentence about each picture using the word "small". Place the paper in his or her binder.

BECAUSE

Have the student _

1. Write the word "because" on an index card.
2. Tape the index card to the poster board.
3. Read the word "because".
4. Choose five index cards and read the words.

Tips to Integrate Technology

1. Type "because" on the computer.
2. Type the sentence: I do not like it because it is small.
3. Print the document and place it in his or her binder.

Tips to Integrate Writing

1. Write "I do not like it because it is small." on the sentence strip.
2. Hang up the sentence strip.
3. Read three sentence strips.

Tips to Motivate the Student

1. Choose words from the left hand column of his or her poster board to read. On the next day, choose words from the right hand column to read. On the following day, choose words from the middle column to read. (This will help prevent the student from reading the same words over and over again!)

MADE

Have the student _

1. Write the word "made" on an index card.
2. Tape the index card to the poster board.
3. Read the word "made".
4. Choose five index cards and read the words.

Tips to Integrate Technology

1. Type "made" on the computer.
2. Type the sentence: Who made the small book?
3. Print the document and place it in his or her binder.

Tips to Integrate Writing

1. Write "Who made the small book?" on the sentence strip.
2. Hang up the sentence strip.
3. Read three sentence strips.

Tips to Differentiate Instruction

1. Explain the difference between a period, an exclamation point, and a question mark. (Periods are used for statements and commands. Exclamation points are used for statements that show strong emotion! Question marks are used for questions.)

Tips to Motivate the Student

1. Make a small book. Write a story using the words he or she has learned.

ABOUT

Have the student _

1. Write the word "about" on an index card.
2. Tape the index card to the poster board.
3. Read the word "about".
4. Choose five index cards and read the words.

Tips to Integrate Technology

1. Type "about" on the computer.
2. Type the sentence: The book is about her school.
3. Print the document and place it in his or her binder.

Tips to Integrate Writing

1. Write "The book is about her school." on the sentence strip.
2. Hang up the sentence strip.
3. Read three sentence strips.

Tips to Differentiate Instruction

1. Read, write, and type the sentence: The book is about his school.
2. Read, write, and type the sentence: The book is about my school.

Tips to Motivate the Student

1. Make a small book. Write a story about his or her school using the words he or she has learned.

ANOTHER

Have the student _

1. Write the word "another" on an index card.
2. Tape the index card to the poster board.
3. Read the word "another".
4. Choose five index cards and read the words.

Tips to Integrate Technology

1. Type "another" on the computer.
2. Type the sentence: I made another book about my family.
3. Print the document and place it in his or her binder.

Tips to Integrate Writing

1. Write "I made another book about my family." on the sentence strip.
2. Hang up the sentence strip.
3. Read three sentence strips.

Tips to Motivate the Student

1. Make another book. Write a story about his or her family using the words he or she has learned.

LOOKING

Have the student _

1. Write the word "looking" on an index card.
2. Tape the index card to the poster board.
3. Read the word "looking".
4. Choose five index cards and read the words.

Tips to Integrate Technology

1. Type "looking" on the computer.
2. Type the sentence: I am looking at another house.
3. Print the document and place it in his or her binder.

Tips to Integrate Writing

1. Write "I am looking at another house." on the sentence strip.
2. Hang up the sentence strip.
3. Read three sentence strips.

Tips to Motivate the Student

1. See how many words he or she can read correctly off of his or her poster board in twenty seconds!

AUTHOR Have

the student _

1. Write the word "author" on an index card.
2. Tape the index card to the poster board.
3. Read the word "author".
4. Choose five index cards and read the words.

Tips to Integrate Technology

1. Type "author" on the computer.
2. Type the sentence: I am the author of the book!
3. Print the document and place it in his or her binder.

Tips to Integrate Writing

1. Write "I am the author of the book!" on the sentence strip.
2. Hang up the sentence strip.
3. Read three sentence strips.

Tips to Motivate the Student

1. Write another book. Title the last page "About the Author" and write a sentence about him or herself.

CAUGHT

Have the student _

1. Write the word "caught" on an index card.
2. Tape the index card to the poster board.
3. Read the word "caught".
4. Choose five index cards and read the words.

Tips to Integrate Technology

1. Type "caught" on the computer.
2. Type the sentence: Her friend caught the ball.
3. Print the document and place it in his or her binder.

Tips to Integrate Writing

1. Write "Her friend caught the ball." on the sentence strip.
2. Hang up the sentence strip.
3. Read three sentence strips.

Tips to Differentiate Instruction

1. Read, write, and type the sentence: His friend caught the ball.
2. Read, write, and type the sentence: My friend caught the ball.
3. Read, write, and type the sentence: Who caught the ball?
4. Read, write, and type the sentence: I caught the ball!

TAUGHT

Have the student _

1. Write the word "taught" on an index card.
2. Tape the index card to the poster board.
3. Read the word "taught".
4. Choose five index cards and read the words.

Tips to Integrate Technology

1. Type "taught" on the computer.
2. Type the sentence: My brother taught me how to play ball.
3. Print the document and place it in his or her binder.

Tips to Integrate Writing

1. Write "My brother taught me how to play ball." on the sentence strip.
2. Hang up the sentence strip.
3. Read three sentence strips.

Tips to Differentiate Instruction

1. Read, write, and type the sentence: Who taught you how to play ball?
2. Read, write, and type the sentence: My sister taught me how to play ball.
3. Read, write, and type the sentence: Dad taught me how to play ball.

Tips to Motivate the Student

1. Teach a younger sibling, friend, or other family member how to do something, such as make a sandwich, play a game, draw a picture, fold the clothes, make a bed, etc. Write a sentence in his or her binder about what he or she taught.

COOK

Have the student ‗

1. Write the word "cook" on an index card.
2. Tape the index card to the poster board.
3. Read the word "cook".
4. Choose seven index cards and read the words.

Tips to Integrate Technology

1. Type "cook" on the computer.
2. Type the sentence: Mom and Dad like to cook.
3. Print the document and place it in his or her binder.

Tips to Integrate Writing

1. Write "Mom and Dad like to cook." on the sentence strip.
2. Hang up the sentence strip.
3. Read three sentence strips.

COOKIE

Have the student ‗

1. Write the word "cookie" on an index card.
2. Tape the index card to the poster board.
3. Read the word "cookie".
4. Choose seven index cards and read the words.

Tips to Integrate Technology

1. Type "cookie" on the computer.
2. Type the sentence: I want another cookie.
3. Print the document and place it in his or her binder.

Tips to Integrate Writing

1. Write "I want another cookie." on the sentence strip.
2. Hang up the sentence strip.
3. Read three sentence strips.

Tips to Motivate the Student

1. Make some cookies with parent or teacher supervision.

COOKBOOK

Have the student _

1. Write the word "cookbook" on an index card.
2. Tape the index card to the poster board.
3. Read the word "cookbook".
4. Choose seven index cards and read the words.

Tips to Integrate Technology

1. Type "cookbook" on the computer.
2. Type the sentence: Who is the author of the cookbook?
3. Print the document and place it in his or her binder.

Tips to Integrate Writing

1. Write "Who is the author of the cookbook?" on the sentence strip.
2. Hang up the sentence strip.
3. Read three sentence strips.

Tips to Motivate the Student

1. Look at a cookbook.

PLAYING

Have the student –

1. Write the word "playing" on an index card.
2. Tape the index card to the poster board.
3. Read the word "playing".
4. Choose seven index cards and read the words.

Tips to Integrate Technology

1. Type "playing" on the computer.
2. Type the sentence: They are playing ball.
3. Print the document and place it in his or her binder.

Tips to Integrate Writing

1. Write "They are playing ball." on the sentence strip.
2. Hang up the sentence strip.
3. Read three sentence strips.

Tips to Differentiate Instruction

1. Complete the sentence "I am playing – " verbally. The parent or teacher may choose this option if the student is unable or learning how to write.
2. Write and complete the sentence "I am playing – "
3. Write a paragraph that begins with the sentence "I am playing – " The parent or teacher may choose this option as an additional enrichment activity.

RIDING

Have the student _

1. Write the word "riding" on an index card.
2. Tape the index card to the poster board.
3. Read the word "riding".
4. Choose seven index cards and read the words.

Tips to Integrate Technology

1. Type "riding" on the computer.
2. Type the sentence: I am riding my new bike.
3. Print the document and place it in his or her binder.

Tips to Integrate Writing

1. Write "I am riding my new bike." on the sentence strip.
2. Hang up the sentence strip.
3. Read three sentence strips.

STORE

Have the student _

1. Write the word "store" on an index card.
2. Tape the index card to the poster board.
3. Read the word "store".
4. Choose seven index cards and read the words.

Tips to Integrate Technology

1. Type "store" on the computer.
2. Type the sentence: They want to go to another store.
3. Print the document and place it in his or her binder.

Tips to Integrate Writing

1. Write "They want to go to another store." on the sentence strip.
2. Hang up the sentence strip.
3. Read three sentence strips.

SHOPPING

Have the student _

1. Write the word "shopping" on an index card.
2. Tape the index card to the poster board.
3. Read the word "shopping".
4. Choose seven index cards and read the words.

Tips to Integrate Technology

1. Type "shopping" on the computer.
2. Type the sentence: They want to go shopping at the mall.
3. Print the document and place it in his or her binder.

Tips to Integrate Writing

1. Write "They want to go shopping at the mall." on the sentence strip.
2. Hang up the sentence strip.
3. Read three sentence strips.

YARD

Have the student _

1. Write the word "yard" on an index card.
2. Tape the index card to the poster board.
3. Read the word "yard".
4. Choose seven index cards and read the words.

Tips to Integrate Technology

1. Type "yard" on the computer.
2. Type the sentence: The yard is next to the house.
3. Print the document and place it in his or her binder.

Tips to Integrate Writing

1. Write "The yard is next to the house." on the sentence strip.
2. Hang up the sentence strip.
3. Read three sentence strips.

Tips to Motivate the Student

1. Draw the front or backyard of his, her, or a family member's house.

CROWN

Have the student _

1. Write the word "crown" on an index card.
2. Tape the index card to the poster board.
3. Read the word "crown".
4. Choose seven index cards and read the words.

Tips to Integrate Technology

1. Type "crown" on the computer.
2. Type the sentence: Her crown is old.
3. Print the document and place it in his or her binder.

Tips to Integrate Writing

1. Write "Her crown is old." on the sentence strip.
2. Hang up the sentence strip.
3. Read three sentence strips.

Tips to Differentiate Instruction

1. Read, write, and type the sentence: His crown is new.

Tips to Motivate the Student

1. Make a crown. Choose a few new words and write the words in glue on the crown. Place craft jewels/gems over the glue to form the words.

FROWN

Have the student ‑

1. Write the word "frown" on an index card.
2. Tape the index card to the poster board.
3. Read the word "frown".
4. Choose seven index cards and read the words.

Tips to Integrate Technology

1. Type "frown" on the computer.
2. Type the sentence: People frown because they are not happy.
3. Print the document and place it in his or her binder.

Tips to Integrate Writing

1. Write "People frown because they are not happy." on the sentence strip.
2. Hang up the sentence strip.
3. Read three sentence strips.

Tips to Differentiate Instruction

1. Read the challenge sentence: Turn that frown upside down!

Tips to Motivate the Student

1. Draw a picture of an upside down frown (a smile).

TOWN

Have the student _

1. Write the word "town" on an index card.
2. Tape the index card to the poster board.
3. Read the word "town".
4. Choose ten index cards and read the words.

Tips to Integrate Technology

1. Type "town" on the computer.
2. Type the sentence: They are going to another town.
3. Print the document and place it in his or her binder.

Tips to Integrate Writing

1. Write "They are going to another town." on the sentence strip.
2. Hang up the sentence strip.
3. Read five sentence strips.

Tips to Motivate the Student

1. Use a map to find another town next to his or her town.

BROWN

Have the student _

1. Write the word "brown" on an index card.
2. Tape the index card to the poster board.
3. Read the word "brown".
4. Choose ten index cards and read the words.

Tips to Integrate Technology

1. Type "brown" on the computer.
2. Type the sentence: She has the brown bike.
3. Print the document and place it in his or her binder.

Tips to Integrate Writing

1. Write "She has the brown bike." on the sentence strip.
2. Hang up the sentence strip.
3. Read five sentence strips.

Tips to Motivate the Student

1. Draw a brown bike.
2. Write the word "brown" with a brown crayon or marker.

TELEVISION

Have the student _

1. Write the word "television" on an index card.
2. Tape the index card to the poster board.
3. Read the word "television".
4. Choose ten index cards and read the words.

Tips to Integrate Technology

1. Type "television" on the computer.
2. Type the sentence: Turn off the television.
3. Print the document and place it in his or her binder.

Tips to Integrate Writing

1. Write "Turn off the television." on the sentence strip.
2. Hang up the sentence strip.
3. Read five sentence strips.

Tips to Differentiate Instruction

1. Draw a small picture of a television over the word "television" to help him or her remember it.

BEACH

Have the student _

1. Write the word "beach" on an index card.
2. Tape the index card to the poster board.
3. Read the word "beach".
4. Choose ten index cards and read the words.

Tips to Integrate Technology

1. Type "beach" on the computer.
2. Type the sentence: The beach is next to his house.
3. Print the document and place it in his or her binder.

Tips to Integrate Writing

1. Write "The beach is next to his house." on the sentence strip.
2. Hang up the sentence strip.
3. Read five sentence strips.

Tips to Differentiate Instruction

1. Read, write, and type the sentence: I wish my friend and I were at the beach.

Tips to Motivate the Student

1. Draw a picture of the beach next to a house.

WEEK EIGHT   DAY THIRTY-NINE

SIT

Have the student _

1. Write the word "sit" on an index card.
2. Tape the index card to the poster board.
3. Read the word "sit".
4. Choose ten index cards and read the words.

Tips to Integrate Technology

1. Type "sit" on the computer.
2. Type the sentence: I always sit next to my best friend.
3. Print the document and place it in his or her binder.

Tips to Integrate Writing

1. Write "I always sit next to my best friend." on the sentence strip.
2. Hang up the sentence strip.
3. Read five sentence strips.

YOUR

Have the student _

1. Write the word "your" on an index card.
2. Tape the index card to the poster board.
3. Read the word "your".
4. Choose ten index cards and read the words.

Tips to Integrate Technology

1. Type "your" on the computer.
2. Type the sentence: Your best friend is riding the bike.
3. Print the document and place it in his or her binder.

Tips to Integrate Writing

1. Write "Your best friend is riding the bike." on the sentence strip.
2. Hang up the sentence strip.
3. Read five sentence strips.

WHY

Have the student _

1. Write the word "why" on an index card.
2. Tape the index card to the poster board.
3. Read the word "why".
4. Choose ten index cards and read the words.

Tips to Integrate Technology

1. Type "why" on the computer.
2. Type the sentence: Why are you looking at another cookbook?
3. Print the document and place it in his or her binder.

Tips to Integrate Writing

1. Write "Why are you looking at another cookbook?" on the sentence strip.
2. Hang up the sentence strip.
3. Read five sentence strips.

ITS

Have the student _

1. Write the word "its" on an index card.
2. Tape the index card to the poster board.
3. Read the word "its".
4. Choose ten index cards and read the words.

Tips to Integrate Technology

1. Type "its" on the computer.
2. Type the sentence: The cat is playing with its ball.
3. Print the document and place it in his or her binder.

Tips to Integrate Writing

1. Write "The cat is playing with its ball." on the sentence strip.
2. Hang up the sentence strip.
3. Read five sentence strips.

Tips to Differentiate Instruction

1. Say, "The word 'its' shows possession. The ball belongs to the cat!"

TOO

Have the student _

1. Write the word "too" on an index card.
2. Tape the index card to the poster board.
3. Read the word "too".
4. Choose ten index cards and read the words.

Tips to Integrate Technology

1. Type "too" on the computer.
2. Type the sentence: My brother is tall too.
3. Print the document and place it in his or her binder.

Tips to Integrate Writing

1. Write "My brother is tall too." on the sentence strip.
2. Hang up the sentence strip.
3. Read five sentence strips.

Tips to Differentiate Instruction

1. Say, "The word 'too' means 'also' or 'more than desired'."
2. Draw a line across the middle section of a piece of paper. Label the top part "too" and label the bottom part "to". Write sentences in each part using the specified word. Place the paper in his or her binder. (Look back over previous sentences for ideas!)

MANY

Have the student _

1. Write the word "many" on an index card.
2. Tape the index card to the poster board.
3. Read the word "many".
4. Choose ten index cards and read the words.

Tips to Integrate Technology

1. Type "many" on the computer.
2. Type the sentence: There are too many people in the store.
3. Print the document and place it in his or her binder.

Tips to Integrate Writing

1. Write "There are too many people in the store." on the sentence strip.
2. Hang up the sentence strip.
3. Read five sentence strips.

WEEK NINE   DAY FORTY-FIVE

BUY

Have the student _

1. Write the word "buy" on an index card.
2. Tape the index card to the poster board.
3. Read the word "buy".
4. Choose ten index cards and read the words.
5. Complete the post-assessment on the next page.

Tips to Integrate Technology

1. Type "buy" on the computer.
2. Type the sentence: I will buy the bike for my friend.
3. Print the document and place it in his or her binder.

Tips to Integrate Writing

1. Write "I will buy the bike for my friend." on the sentence strip.
2. Hang up the sentence strip.
3. Read five sentence strips.

POST-ASSESSMENT

# of words identified correctly: +

Parent/Teacher Instructions: Write the student's favorite hobby by #1. Check off each word the student read correctly. Write the number of words the student read correctly in the box above. Compare the number of words the student is able to read now to the number of words the student read on the pre-assessment.

Student Instructions: Read the words you recognize in each column.

1.	16. small	31. shopping
2. always	17. because	32. yard
3. next	18. made	33. crown
4. friend	19. about	34. frown
5. people	20. another	35. town
6. family	21. looking	36. brown
7. turn	22. author	37. television
8. around	23. caught	38. beach
9. off	24. taught	39. sit
10. light	25. cook	40. your
11. found	26. cookie	41. why
12. best	27. cookbook	42. its
13. don't	28. playing	43. too
14. wish	29. riding	44. many
15. cold	30. store	45. buy

Parent/Teacher Disclaimer: Please note the pre-assessment and post-assessment are informal assessments. Neither assessment is meant to be a formal or diagnostic test.

ABOUT THE AUTHOR

S. V. Richard is a special educator and raises three daughters.

Ingram Content Group UK Ltd.
Milton Keynes UK
UKHW050959060723
424661UK00013B/264